No Constant Hues

No Constant Hues

Poems

by Eleanor Berry

Copyright © 2015 Eleanor Berry

All rights reserved. No part of this work may be reproduced or transmitted in any form or by any means, electronic or mechanical, or by any information storage or retrieval system, except as may be expressly permitted by the publisher.

Cover art: *Old Growth, Marys Peak Wilderness*
Watercolor by Robin Christy Humelbaugh
Used by permission

Author photo and cover by Richard Berry
Book design and layout by Eleanor Berry

Turnstone Books of Oregon, LLC
Seal Rock, OR

Printed in the United States of America

ISBN 978-0692323199

ACKNOWLEDGMENTS

Grateful acknowledgment is made to the editors of the following publications, in which the listed poems first appeared, some in different versions.

Adanna: "Fire All Around"
Breathe: 101 Contemporary Odes, ed. Ryan G. Van Cleave & Chad Prevost (C & R Press, 2009): "Ode in Shades of Green"
Concord 5 (2013), eds. Sandra Ellston & Ruth F. Harrison: "Found Objects"
Dogwood: "Where Her Mother Had Placed It"
Gingko Tree Review: "Inland from the Edge
Imagination & Place: Seasoning, ed. Kelly Barth (Imagination & Place Press, 2010): "Nettlesome"
Just before Igniting (The Peregrine Writers, 2003): "Taking the Field"
The MacGuffin: "Not to Buy"
Moving Mountain: "Small Repair"
The Portland Pen (newsletter of the NLAPW Portland, OR, Branch): "Their Surfaces, Their Whirrings"
Prairie Schooner: "Grotesques," "In Praise of Proprioception"
Verseweavers: The Oregon State Poetry Association Anthology of Prize-Winning Poems: "Bright Fingers," "Night Soil," "Wild Gardens"
Windfall: A Journal of Poetry of Place: "Where Gravity Has Brought Them"

"Inland from the Edge" has been reprinted in *Concord* 5 (2013), eds. Sandra Ellston & Ruth F. Harrison.

"Taking the Field" has been reprinted in *Visiting Dr. Williams: Poems Inspired by the Life and Work of William Carlos Williams*, ed. Thom Tammaro & Sheila Coghill (University of Iowa Press, 2011).

"A Fascicle from Shotpouch Creek" derives from a brief collaborative residency, with Richard Berry, at the Cabin at Shotpouch Creek, as part of a program of the Spring Creek Project, Department of Philosophy, Oregon State University.

Thanks to my fellow poets in The Peregrine Writers—Marilyn Johnston, Stephanie Lenox, Ada Molinoff, Lois Rosen, Colette Tennant, Dina Triest, and the late Virginia Corrie-Cozart—for their critques of earlier versions of many of these poems and for the inspiration of their own poetry.

Thanks to Robin Christy Humelbaugh for the generous spirit of her art and for her willingness to join a painting of hers with these poems of mine.

Thanks to Sandra Mason and Ruth F. Harrison for their support of my work, and to Charles Goodrich, Lex Runciman, and Lisa M. Steinman for the time and care they gave to reading the entire manuscript of this book.

Deepest thanks to my husband, Richard Berry, who has accompanied and supported me in every phase of the making of this book and of all my poetry.

For Richard,
always with me in
*these wild fields where
we study flowers, observe the stars*

CONTENTS

I. Their Surfaces, Their Whirrings
    Grotesques   3
    The Scent of Crushed Fir   5
    Power Outage   6
    Their Surfaces, Their Whirrings   8
    Like Linens in Drawers   10
    Where Her Mother Had Placed It   11
    Hanging the New Picture   12
    The Potter's Studio   13
    Flight   14
    Gift   15
    Guest Cottage   17
    Trunk   18
    Found Objects   19
    Anniversary   20

II. Small Repair
    Bucolics   25
    Night Soil   28
    Riverstone   30
    Small Repair   31
    Not to Buy   33
    A Fascicle from Shotpouch Creek   35

III. Taking the Field
    Wild Gardens   45
    Perennials   46
    Why Praise Aconites?   47
    I'll Take These   49
    By Feel   51
    Under the Trees   53
    White against Dark   54
    Circle, Triangle, Square   56
    Nettlesome   57
    Air on Skin   59
    Windows Overlooking Gardens   60
    Ode in Shades of Green   61

Taking the Field	64
Where Gravity Has Brought Them	65

IV. Transit
High Desert Abecedarius	69
Transit	74
Island Daybook	76

V. Bright Fingers
Foothill Route	81
Softly Out of the Dark	82
Where I Left Off	85
Lines for a Mother-in-law	87
Fire All Around	89
Inland from the Edge	91
The Music He Made	95
Voices of Birds	96
Bright Fingers	99
Floral Study	101
Left to Me	103
The Trail Down	104
The Wear	105
In Praise of Proprioception	107
What Will You Take?	108
The Shapes of Their Bodies	110

About the Poet	113
About the Artist	113
About this Book	114

I
Their Surfaces, Their Whirrings

Grotesques

Flying cross-country, I peer
out the cabin window
six miles down at the skin
of the planet,
its roughness smoothed
by that depth of air, but
its swelling, pitting, splitting
visible still at this distance.

From that porthole view of Earth
as a relief map of itself, my gaze
swings to my hands, erupted from barely
brushing poison ivy, pocked like the top
of a pancake ready to flip, like the crust
of Earth, upheaved in peaks and ridges.

Above me, on three screens, spaced
the length of the aisle, *The Fantastic Four*
pass through an interplanetary storm
of special effects, emerge transformed—
the bald one's skin now fissured stone,
the woman's body turning
at tense moments to invisible vapor,
her suitor's arms and legs
flowing in streams, the last ablaze
from his own heat—as if
in each, a single one
of the four classical elements
had been distilled
from the otherwise indissoluble
mix of all. The quartet
of astronauts annealed
into earth, air, water, and fire:
four superheroes, four grotesques.

Flight attendants, bringing coffee
and packaged snacks, recoil
at the sight of my hands, blistered skin
oozing and scabbing. Transformed
by the touch of a leaf, I, too,
have become a grotesque. And Earth,
however tranquil it appears
beneath the plane, is spawn
of the violence of stars, its elements
fused in their fierce heats, its core
still molten, eruptive, its crust
cracked, Titans' spherical puzzle of colliding,
rebounding pieces, tirelessly transforming itself.

The Scent of Crushed Fir

Commuting to work while the highway was being widened, every day I watched yellow dinosaur brushmowers hack and maul the limbs of giant trees, devour slim trunks whole. Bulldozers dug out Titans' heads, huge stumps ringed with shaggy locks of roots, shoved them into mountainous slash-piles. For months the highway was a route through devastation. Every morning and evening, on the way to work and on the way back home, I breathed the scent of crushed fir.

~

The windstorm this February arrived unannounced, spent its fury in an hour. It strewed our woods-hemmed lawn with fir-limbs the size of saplings, laid eight thick fir-trunks across our neighbors' drive, flung high-voltage power-lines across all four lanes of the highway, blew out windows of nearby houses, tore off the sheet-metal roof of a post office up the canyon, and left thousands of people without power for days.

The sudden tempest felled trees in swathes, as if they were cornstalks. It ripped open the canopy that had shaded and sheltered the plants of the understory. Driving the dark highway soon after the power company crews had cleared it of downed wires, I glimpsed, just beyond the headlights' cones of brightness, shadowy mounds of tree limbs heaped along the shoulders. For miles, I breathed the scent of crushed fir.

Power Outage

Habitable space shrank
to a tight half-circle
in front of the wood-stove.
All day a kettle
hissed on the cast-iron stove-top.

After supper we sat with our tea—
you in the rocker, quilt
wrapping your shoulders,
I in the wing chair,
afghan over my knees.
The walls of the room
receded into darkness, broken
only by stray gleams—
candlelight reflected
off the glass on framed pictures.

The semicircle where we sat
close to the stove, warming
cold fingers against
steaming mugs, became
a clearing in a forest, looming
about us, alien, familiar.

You tuned our battery-powered radio
to public television
for *The NewsHour with Jim Lehrer*.
Then we listened
to Baroque horn concertos
on our old portable tape player,
till a belt broke and the reels
stopped turning.

The third night, we kept the radio
on Channel 7 for *Frontline*.
A Canadian journalist was recounting

how she'd travelled Iran incognito,
interviewing dissidents, when the power
came back on. Beneath us,
the furnace started up. Around us,
the forest leapt back.

We sat in brightness, still listening
to the journalist's voice. At last
I picked up the remote, turned
the TV on. Its screen lit up with a picture.
The voice that had come to us
out of the darkness now came
from a face with definite features.

The forest was gone. The room,
bright to its corners.

Their Surfaces, Their Whirrings

Things are in the saddle and ride mankind.
— Ralph Waldo Emerson

Here, packed into one kitchen drawer,
instructions and owners' manuals
for nearly all the appliances and
household utensils we've ever owned:
toasters and coffeemakers
that have pre-deceased us;
a vacuum cleaner long since
dead too; the dehumidifier that gasped its last
earlier this year, most likely outliving
its first owner, the elderly neighbor
who handed it down when he moved
to a retirement home
some twenty years back.

Jumbled here with those dead,
others still alive—the washer and dryer,
pushing thirty now, that stood, new and unscuffed,
white enamel gleaming under weak
basement-window light,
in the first house we owned;
the turntable that still plays
our miscellaneous assortment
of classical records, top-heavy with Bach;
the small oscillating fan, bought a few summers ago
to replace another, whose motor had failed; our new
indoor/outdoor thermometer, successor
to one whose readings suddenly went wild.

I think we know ourselves
in part by these things
we call ours. We spend our days
in their midst. Daily their surfaces
greet our glances, our touch. Their whirrings
accompany our speech, even our thought.

When we neglect them, they demand
our guilty attention. They ride us all right.

But we fill them so much with ourselves, they swell
into steeds we can ride in our turn, till even
these mere brochures and instruction sheets bear me
across years upon years of our intertwined lives.

Like Linens in Drawers

I beat and beat the whites to light foam, then fold
them into the sauce, fearful I'll deflate them by an extra
    fold.

Not only paper, but, under stress, even rock,
if it does not break, ever so slowly folds.

A wet gust in the middle of August, then a chill
week of rain, as if the cycle of seasons could fold.

There on the busy sidewalk, a young couple hugs. Old love,
youth has left us, which now their arms enfold.

Five years teaching at the college, I took it for home.
Fired, I saw it anew, from outside the fold.

Like wings of pale, night-flying moths, in my friend's
garden at dusk, petals of evening primrose unfold.

In this book of Hafiz, Persian text and English—one
running left; the other, right—face each other across
    the fold.

Before she gave it to me, Eleanor was my mother's name,
never used, like the linens she kept in drawers, never
    unfolded.

Where Her Mother Had Placed It

An aptness for arranging objects,
each beautiful in itself, but more
or differently so when placed among the rest,

even things ugly in themselves, pleasing
only when brought together
in a particular configuration—

this talent or obsession, she thinks,
fidgeting with a bowl, a lamp,
and a pair of books on a table, is what

she most took from her mother, is where
she undeniably recognizes her mother
in herself—in the movements of her hands,

squarish like her father's but, shifting
a candle and a vase on the top of a bookcase,
moving as her mother's long-fingered ones moved,

which had seemed, like her mother's long,
graceful legs, beside her own thick-ankled
short ones, remoter than the features

of ancestors, painted by other ancestors,
gazing from their portraits on the walls
down at her, their unlikely descendant,

while she dusted as her mother had told her,
putting each object she touched
back where her mother had placed it.

Hanging the New Picture

    for Amy Wagner

To make a spot for your "Moon over Angel Valley," I move
the print of November from the *Très riches heures* from over
the little white bookcase in the living room to beside
the dresser in the bedroom, where the small O'Keeffe
    petunia
and Diebenkorn seated woman prints have been; take
the petunia to the hall under the doorbell chimes and
Sue Allen's pileated woodpeckers from under the chimes
and her vanilla leaf from over the desk in the dining room
to the hall beside the coat closet, where the sprig-
    embroidered
bell pull has hung, move the bell pull to the guest bathroom
and the seated woman to the place above the desk
in the dining room, where the vanilla leaf was before.

Some months ahead, I'll move most all again—then see
the serried mountain ridges that step above your valley,
the aureoled stars and fat crescent moon that blazon
its black nighttime sky, afresh, in a new spot.

The Potter's Studio

is built against a hill beside his house.
The back and one side nestle against the hill.
The front opens a door to visitors who come
to see his pots in the place they're made.
The other side looks out
wide windows toward a wooded yard.

Through cloud or fog, through fir boughs
and streaked panes, daylight filters
down into the studio. It carries the azure
of sky above clouddeck or fogbank, the deep
teal of firs, umber of bark, emerald
of salal and swordfern. It carries
wisps of rose—from the ragged edge
of a cloud where the sun
breaks through, from the glow on the far
horizon where it sinks.

                        In the still air
of the studio, those mountain-forest colors
settle on the white clay sides of the vases,
planters, and bowls that the potter lifts
from the wheel, till every glazed vessel
is a landscape, is a world
of earth and trees and sky
two hands can hold.

Flight

> *Tulip Expansion* (acrylics, 2004),
> by John Larimer

You lift your brush to paint
Incipience, tight-furled,
pointed bud, petals' promised fire
still wholly sheathed
in sepals' green. But even

as you start to paint, that
slim finial sags
to plump egg, that green
ruddies. Now it's
Readiness you're painting.

And well before you're done,
that flushed, swollen
tulip bud will crack
soundlessly open, spread
rose-orange wings.

Gift

> for Paulann Petersen

Never a mother, I was startled
at your Mother's Day gift of flowers—
four stargazer lilies, many-branched stalks
thick with buds, the first rose-pink
six-pointed star barely flared open;
three tall callas, cream-white spathes
still tightly furled; all set off by green salal.

Day after day, for ten days, lilies and callas
opened and opened in the amethyst-glass
pitcher on the mantelpiece. Now
two callas' spread spathes turn
brown at the edge; their green stems
bend lower and lower, finally fracture
under the weight of those heavy blooms.

Now lilies drop their petals in small,
purplish-pink heaps on the mantel,
on the Franklin stove's cast-iron top,
on the hearth-rug below, where the dog
sniffs at them, puzzled. Limp petals,
spent anthers, a blasted bud—I scoop them up,
drop them by handfuls into the compost.

The single calla still intact I gently pull
from the pitcher, cut fresh its stem,
and set it, solitary bloom, displaying
its elegant form, diffusing
its delicate scent, in a green-gold
wine bottle on the sill above the kitchen sink.
Mornings, I'll see it backlit in the rising sun.

Weeks or months later, I'll dig dark
fertile muck from the bottom
of the composter, spade it deep

into a garden bed. There I'll plant
bulbs of lilies, prime among them
pink stargazer—fragrant cultivar,
summer-blooming, I'll rename *Paulann's gift*.

Guest Cottage

    for Marion Davidson

As house cats do in new surroundings, I've sniffed
around the edges of these small rooms, found a spot
where I can sit surveying the whole—here, stretched
pillow-propped on the sofa. Snug against this corner,
facing the door, I can take in all the spaces
of the cottage with one easy swing of my gaze.

I like the simple floor-plan: living room running the
    length
of this remodelled garage and half its width; the other
    half
split into kitchen, bath, and an alcove just big enough
for an old double bed with a bookshelf headboard—
same design as my husband's and mine. If I want
a high roost, there's a ladder I can climb to a loft.

I like the colors, too—the same shades of orange and
    brown
on these sofa pillows, on the bed's coverlet and quilt,
as on the upholstered footstool my husband saved
from the sale of his parents' household goods.
It matched their sofa, but looks as much at home
in our living room, where nothing matches anything
    else.

No cat, I've taken decades to feel at home in this body,
in the garments—new, used, discount, and inherited—
that I combine to clothe it, and the furnishings, no less
miscellaneous, that I arrange around it, or take delight
in finding already arranged as I might have, in spaces
my imagination might have built to house itself.

Trunk

> *Do not save love*
>   *for things*
>   *Throw* things
>   *to the flood*
>   – Lorine Niedecker

"Get rid of things!" I urge you, but the trunk
I took to college remains. Brass-edged, its shallow
partitioned tray removed, it's a card, "blank
inside," that we've filled with our own message, howl

proclaiming our presence, ourselves its heavy cargo—
the places we've lived, our friends, each other, in picture
upon picture, mounted black-and-white, the slow
silver emulsion a vial holding a tincture

of the fields we walked, summer and winter, memory
of cooking cabbage, its smell filling the room
we rented on Brunswick, string-trellised morning glory
overtopping our roof, the trolley's warning tune.

For all my efforts to cast them off, the things
we've lived among, even when gone, still cling.

Found Objects

> *We choose such objects for some turn of grace*
> *we'd like to own forever, close at hand*
> *as lovers, though unwarm, unsentient, and*
> *though statements they might make are made in place.*
> — Ruth F. Harrison, from *"objets d'art"*

We choose such objects for some turn of grace,
felicity of form that draws our glance
to linger, imagination to attach
itself, for something about them that by chance
resembles treasures lost we've longed to match.
We choose such objects for some turn of grace

we'd like to own forever, close at hand
as the cat curled each morning on our lap,
as music sounding deep within our chest
long after it's ceased. We choose what fills a gap
we'd scarcely felt, those few among the rest
we'd like to own forever, close at hand

as lovers, though unwarm, unsentient, and
inert. They keep us faithful company,
greet our arrival home, dispel our fear
of loneliness. In sunlight, lamplight, we see
their character come clear. They soon grow dear
as lovers, though unwarm, unsentient, and

though statements they might make are made in place
and without words, without expressive sound
or signifying gesture. They are the chorus
for the private drama of our days, profound
despite their quiet. They speak both to and for us
though statements they might make are made in place.

Anniversary

Hung the length of the deck rail, the curtains
billow in the warm, early-June breeze.
Unpacked from damp storage, rank with mildew,
they're out here to air—curtains
from nearly every window of every house
we lived in before this one—three decades
of our life together, beginning with the red burlap,
long since faded, then the burgundy and the purple,
colorfast and permapress, each pair hand-sewed
before I learned that, to cover a window when closed,
curtains must be twice its width.

The rest, readymades—at first, what we could afford
on your wages for day labor and mine as a typist,
then on our grad school assistantships.
The coarse cornflower-print that we hung
in the tall kitchen window of the flat
on Albany Avenue, and must have bought
from Honest Ed's, is gone. But here's
the lined chintz—its big, stylized blossoms,
red, gold, royal blue, and brown, bedizened
the living room's only window, looking out
onto the sidewall of the duplex next door.

These loose-woven drapes the color of straw—
in the small house we rented
a long commute from Toronto, they framed
the picture-window facing its poplar-filled
deep front yard. This narrow pair, in the same
soft, tawny cloth, hung in the side window.
The one day we didn't pull them open
at our usual time, the owners phoned
from their bigger house on the acre beside us
to check—were we all right?

No Constant Hues

These daisy-sprigged, ruffled café curtains
are faded in swaths—bleached by sunlight spilled
from over the roof-peak of the tall two-story
shadowing our one-floor Milwaukee bungalow
down to the windows over our kitchen sink.
These white sheers, with butterflies
embroidered on their borders, hung above
the long plywood desk you built
in the spare bedroom we took for our study.
All winter, the windowpanes glimmering
behind them were damasked with frost.

Far from those windows they once adorned,
here in the spring breeze, curtains belly like spinnakers
all along the deck rail. They lift in the warm wind
together—cottons, sheers, ruffled, plain—curtains
that used to hang in nearly all the rooms
that once were ours. They lift and wave
from the deck rail like pennants, as if this house
were hung with banners, in celebration, as if
it were a new ship, embarking.

II
Small Repair

Bucolics

While we're eating breakfast, the small herd
in our pasture gathers at the back fence.
Four cows, two calves, stand looking in at us
as we look out at them.

The black calf bends his neck, tips his head
almost upside down, and stretches his long,
thick, pinkish-gray tongue
to lick the dog-chain draped on a fence post.

~

Every day the herd in our pasture
meets at the fence with our neighbors'
larger herd. They stand for a long time
face to face, as if comparing notes.

~

Perched with our dog on the brow
of the hill overlooking
the neighbors' pasture, while their cows
graze close below, in the stillness I hear
grass stalks rip.

~

The new calf watches as I approach
with the dog, staggers up and starts toward us.

Low moo from the mother,
warning the bold one back.

~

Whenever the winter cloudcover gives way
to sun, the cows lie out in the open,
chewing cud, dark hides absorbing
brief warmth.

                    Hot August afternoons,
they couch in the shade of a lone fir
or deep in the shadowy woodlot. Rousing
one by one, heaving themselves up,
they browse lower branches,
rub neck and flanks on rough bark.

At dark, they gather for sleep
out of the wind, returning to the same place
several nights in a row, then choosing
a new shelter. They don't come back to the old spot
till their dung has decayed and the grass recovered.

~

When we pick apples from the overgrown tree
on our side of the fence, the entire neighbor herd—
cows, heifers, last spring's calves—
gallop from across the pasture
up to the fence to watch. Wide-eyed, drooling,
they wait for us to throw them windfalls.

~

Sheltering from the downpour, the cows
lie close together beneath a great fir's
umbrella boughs. Recumbent, each massive body

has exactly the form of the small carved cow
I remember from childhood—I could hold it
between thumb and forefinger.

Each spine bends
in the same curve
as my finger would trace.

~

Dead, the pregnant cow
lies rolled from her left side
halfway onto her back.
Legs stick out stiffly.

No Constant Hues

Limp tail drags in dew-soaked grass.
Belly looms, pale and swollen
as a full moon.
From the distended udder, teats stretch
for the unborn calf.

When I pulled open the curtains,
there she was in the neighbors' pasture,
her ungainly dead body
straight below the bedroom window.

Now the neighbors come with their pick-up,
hoist her aboard. The grass
flattened beneath her weight
slowly springs back.

Night Soil

1

Today the world is the heft
of bale after bale of weedy, mixed-grass hay.
It's pin-jabs from cut ends
of grass stalks and weed stems, bristling
everywhere from each twine-bound bulk
we bear-hug onto the stack.

It's barbs of innumerable awns
piercing our pants and socks,
lodging in skin.
It's the sweetness distilled
of orchard grass and clover
dried in hot sun.

It's pollen-heavy clouds
of fine hay-dust, particles
inhaled with every breath, coating
our nostrils and throats.

Today the world insists
it is there, harsh and sweet,
right up against us,
penetrant.

2

Today the world is the density
of wet, compacted cow dung
on the blade of the shovel
as I load the big wheelbarrow
over and over
with the dark leavings in the barn.

It's the weight of each load
dragging against my arms

as I wheel it, bouncing
over rocky, rutted ground,
to the slowly building berm
of rotting manure.

It's the sweet stench
I keep smelling all day,
long after I've left off digging,
washed, and changed—
stink of excrement, tinged still
with the sweetness of fresh hay,

feed for bull-calves confined
to paddock and barn.
It's the darkness
of the spreading pool
in which they stood to feed,
lay to sleep.

It's the darkness
of their blood dried
on the ground where it spilled
slick and red.

It's the darkness
of night soil, offal
from sweet grass feed, turned
to compost for new crops.

Riverstone

One of thousands hereabout,
strewn across pasture and woodlot
or still held fast
in the earth beneath—
stones left behind
when the ancient river shifted course.

Months back, a cow's hard hoof
knocked it loose
from fir roots that had gripped it
tightly for decades, as they laced
the gravelly soil. Since then,
it's lain half-hidden in grass
where the hoof's blow lodged it.

Now a woman lifts it from the ground.
Hefting its weight, she cups palm,
wraps fingers, close around
its stream-tumbled form.
She holds it almost
tenderly, as if admiring
what a smooth globe
rushing waters made it, or how,
in its dense solidity,
it simply is.

To be so lifted and held, to receive
such gentle attention—
a rock picked, perhaps,
to edge a flowerbed or to mark
the grave of a dog, who
walked here with her
daily for years—

Small Repair

This steep bank was cut in three days and three nights of rain in February 1996. As the downpour continued without letup, our small seasonal creek grew to a torrent that rushed downhill, tearing rocks and boulders from the pastureland beside it, digging its channel deeper and deeper.

Every day, heavy cows lurched down the bank and clambered back, dislodging rocks with their hooves; calves cantered down and scrambled up, loosing showers of stones. Under this wear, part of the bank collapsed in a rockslide.

After several years, the farmer who pastured his small herd on our land fell ill and sold off the last of his cows.

On the steep bank, seeds hurled from exploding pods of Scotch broom sprouted and grew. Canes of Himalayan blackberry straddled the creek, and their tips took root, starting new plants, which sent up new canes. Spindrift seeds of cat's-ear thrust taproots down between pebbles and cobbles, spread broad rosettes of coarse leaves.

~

Now, eight years after floodwaters cut it, we've come, you and I, to reclaim this gravelly steep from the weeds, to hold it against further erosion:

Bracing on rocks in the dry creekbed, I reach up with the pole pruner, hook it at the base of thick blackberry canes, pull its blade through fresh wood and dead, then tug the tangled lengths of thorny severed canes down off the slope. You reach from the top with the pole saw, draw it back and forth, cutting through woody stalks of broom. Then you rope the springy bushes together, haul them up the bank.

I clamber up where the steepness eases, pulling out broom plants young enough that their roots are not yet deeply wedged in the rocks. With every step, the gravelly soil gives way under my feet. Each time I wrench a root free, a small stream of sand and pebbles rattles down the slope.

As the massive web of blackberry and the dense overgrowth of broom are thinned away, modest native plants appear: A ragged line of maple saplings dances along a narrow shelf, branches bent akimbo by the weight of canes that draped them. A slender fir seedling, rooted midway up the slope, points straight skyward. Green plumes of swordfern ray out from scattered niches.

Working from the top with a string trimmer, I scythe the tall grass growing on the crest of the slope and spreading down its face. As this shaggy beard is shaved, the contours of the bank emerge at last, in detail.

You dig a trench along the crest, insert one end of a thirty-foot strip of loose-woven jute, refill, and tamp. With its top secure, you throw its length over the slope, then climb down a ladder beside it, patting the coarse netting close against the ground. Last, you poke the prongs of six-inch staples down among the rocks, to pin the jute in place.

~

Over the next several weeks, we'll lay some twenty strips of jute side by side against the steep bank, to hold the soil from slipping. Then, late in the winter, we'll pound in cuttings and plug in seedlings of native shrubs, to spread a network of roots that can hold it firmly and long.

In Earth's tattered cover, we make a small repair.

Not to Buy

On the radio, reporters describe
how work crews scoop and sift and pass
pail after pail of debris from the collapsed twin towers.
Three thousand miles west, I gently scrub
with paper towels moistened in alcohol
the schefflera's scale-crusted leaves and stems.

As the newscasters announce
a national day of prayer,
I push the blade of the spatula
along the grain of the wood
of our old bedstead, coated with stripper,
lifting swaths of softened paint.

As the President's message is broadcast
and re-broadcast on the hour
and half-hour all afternoon,
Go back to your lives, buy,
fly, take the family
to Disney World, don't let the terrorists

think they've destroyed
the American way of life,
I stroke the hardened first coat
of varnish on the refinished bedstead
with quadruple-zero steel wool,
feeling the surface grow smooth.

I remember how Sara and Rodrigo,
my young friends, folded paper into cranes
as gifts to all the guests
at their wedding. I want
not to buy, but to make and to give,
to use, re-use, refurbish.

I want to bring in logs
cut from the bigleaf maple that fell
in last year's windstorm.
I want to ask friends
to sit with me in the warmth
of all its rings of growth.

I want to pile worn riverstones
into retaining walls and seed the crevices
with native larkspur and phlox.
I want to place stones on sand
so they hold nothing
but are beautiful.

I want to make poems, using
old words, rounded as riverstones,
and present them as gifts. I want to fold pages
of poems that fly, and slip them
into hands of sad-faced strangers. I want to raise
no flag but a leaf.

A Fascicle from Shotpouch Creek
13-16 May 2008

I

So many thorny and spiny plants—
    salmonberry, stinging nettle—
        such tall, vigorous stands

border the meadow, crowd
    the creekside trail, thicket
        the lower slopes, it seems

this wild place
    hedges itself
        against intruders

So rank the growth
    of stinging nettle, the very smell
        repels, the stink

of formic acid
    each brushed spine
        secretes, which burns on touch

        ~

Robust, shoulder-high,
    these larkspur on the brink
        of bloom

dispel any notion
    all spring wildflowers
        are delicate

        ~

A bewilderment
    of leaves, uncountably
        many, each elaborately

cut, lobed, toothed—
    waterleaf, mitrewort,
        blanketing the ditchbank

            ~

Soaring alders
    still let light reach
        this forest floor

Until their crowns fill out
    these steeps will stay
        knee-deep in green

flocked with pale
    tiny flowers—
        sorrel, miner's lettuce, bleeding heart

            ~

As if by art, these
    rhizomatous herbs
        spread broad mats

gracefully butted and lapped
    over the land's
        hollows and slopes

Beneath the leaves'
    jostle for sun, underground stems
        thread with no shuttle

the gravelly soil, push
    down from their nodes
        anchoring roots, crisscross to weave

hidden nets—ever-expanding warp
    for floral rugs more elaborate
        than any artist could hook

No Constant Hues

~

Close up, intricate,
    symmetrical forms appear
        even in such

inconspicuous blooms
    as these greenish and purplish
        pendants no bigger than dewdrops

Along this stalk, each
    is a dollhouse serving dish, delicacies
        tidily ranged in a circlet,

on that one, all tiny pitchers
    tipped to pour—
        forms so completely distinct

once they've been seen
    it's suddenly
        easy to distinguish

species from kindred
    species, mitrewort from
        piggyback plant, however much alike

their round-lobed leaves
    and habit of growth
        It's suddenly

easy to part
    staminate from pistillate
        flowers of meadowrue—

Lilliputians' fringed lampshades
    from their fancy hats—
        on otherwise identical separate plants

~

Small, three-lobed calyces,
        purplish-brown, peer from under
                the wild ginger's

mantling leaves,
        repeat in modest miniature
                the showy trilliums'

large, three-petalled corollas,
        now, from age,
                purpled, shrunk, and curled

~

Between the trillium
        blossoms' withering
                and the larkspurs'

budding out,
        the season trembles,
                then tumbles

almost into summer
        Sun routs for now
                the legions of cloud

Sky blazes blue
        High in the canopy, new leaves
                begin to patch a shade

II

Logged, logged again, then
        a new plan—restore
                the ancient forest

This, with red alder and big-leaf maple
    the dominant species,
        a stage on the way

to a climax of conifers
    Bacteria living
        in the roots of the alders

fix nitrogen, enrich
    the soil for seedlings—
        hemlock, redcedar, Douglas fir

    ~

Tyee Formation, the soil in which
    this forest takes root—
        sands and siltstones washed,

some forty million
    years back, from the ancient
        Klamath Mountains down

into the Pacific, forming
    a submarine fan, then
        repeatedly dislodged and laid

down again by earthquake, making
    new layerings—telltale
        turbidites, fine grains atop coarse

Quake-prone still, this land
    accreted to the continent
        in the Eocene

as rugged Sichuan, even now shaken
    by repeated shocks, steeps
        collapsing into rubble

~

In Sichuan now, botanists
    monitor bamboo, fearful
        it will not hold

steady to its slow cycle
    of blooming only once
        every seventy-odd years,

but flower and die *en masse*—
    as swaths of it did three decades back
        after the province's last

powerful quake—leaving
    endangered giant pandas
        scarce browse

~

Ten times older
    than this Coast Range
        creekside where it thrives,

the common horsetail—common
    in wetlands worldwide,
        species scarcely changed

from Carboniferous forests
    where herbivorous dinosaurs
        browsed its tree-size kin,

survivor of late-Cretaceous
    meteor impacts that
        killed off both

those giant breeds, along with most other
    plant and animal kinds
        then inhabiting Earth—

anachronism among
    the angiosperms that now
        hold sway among plants

the planet round, "living fossil"
    some three hundred million
        years old

    ~

Each hollow horsetail stem
    petrified alive—
        silica filling

the walls of its cells
    Now, before the green
        barren stems emerge,

sprouting in whorls
    branches thin and pliant
        as pine needles,

gaggles of whitish
    fertile stalks
        poke through the grass

club-like heads, each one ringed
    with dots of stalked discs,
        under each disc

a band of sporangia—microscopic
    forms that appear
        only in close-up, as

when boiling water is poured
    into the glass teacup, the tiny
        fascicle of tea-leaves

swells and releases,
>   like a miniature parachute,
>   >   its string-bound "flower"

CODA

How to see
>   plants conspicuous here,
>   >   their thorny thickets,

spiny stands—as
>   forbidding entry
>   >   or inviting study

Coastal tribes knew
>   even nettles provide
>   >   stalks palatable steamed

or steeped for spring tonic,
>   and fiber to weave
>   >   sturdy fishnets and snares,

knew salmonberry offers
>   early each spring
>   >   delectable green sprouts

to peel and eat raw,
>   magenta-petalled blossoms, brightening
>   >   brush still winter-drear,

and, best, amid persistent blooms,
>   earliest berries—welcome sweet
>   >   to garnish salmon and nourish

migrant thrushes—*salmonberry birds*,
>   whose song proclaims
>   >   berries are ripe

III
Taking the Field

Wild Gardens

> *These hedge-rows, hardly hedge-rows, little lines*
> *Of sportive wood run wild . . .*
>   – William Wordsworth

It's not mowed lawns, tilled fields, weedless pastures,
or woodlots cleared of brush that have drawn me
ever since childhood, when the space beneath
an unpruned forsythia was my favorite refuge. It's
fields grown over with alder, hawthorne, apple and pear
gone wild, asters and goldenrod. It's woodland left to itself,
patches and pockets of wildness, that I've loved.

It's words like *thicket, bush,* names for dense growth,
hodgepodge variety of grasses, wildflowers, shrubs,
small trees—natives and invasives together—sprung
from seed carried on the coats of deer, fox, coyote,
or planted with their scat. Just so much *wilderness*
as the "Wilderness Park Area" outside town—strip
of swampy woods with a trail for walkers, dogs on leash.

It's woods just big enough for me to get lost in—
until my father found me or the dog, given his head,
led me out—or to feel smug when I don't. It's sentences
that extend and interrupt themselves over and over,
unpredictably, as a trail is lost in lush grass
growing faster than the few hikers can flatten it,
but, beyond the wet meadow, picks up again.

It's the outdoor rooms I've entered with no need to knock,
remnants of gardens in places gone wild, what had been
    a lawn
with shrub borders, ornamental trees, now a sudden
    clearing
in woods, where surviving hybrids bloom among
vigorous stock that asks no tending. It's stanzas
the language at once bends into and bursts beyond,
gardens whose makers welcome self-sown wildings.

Perennials

    for John Larimer

A few lank roots from your garden, still clutching
grains of its rich soil: last fall I dug them
into the earth of mine. Now this
sprawl of panicled branches, bent, erect, recumbent,
this haze of violet lifting
from the spent flowerbed like mist over the river at dawn.

You call them *Michaelmas daisies*. I've always called them
asters, happy to think, with that name
the candelabra of their small compound flowers
must be *asterisms*—and they are, glowing
as much in autumn gloom
as bright star clusters in a dark night sky.

Flowering perennials—we name them for what we see
in their blossoms, what their blooming seems to match
on our calendars: *Michaelmas daisies*, as if they opened,
like daylilies mysteriously brought into phase, all
for just one day, St. Michael's
late-September feast day. But even cut,
they last for weeks. So that name must simply reflect
they're at their peak around the end of September—

as *oceanspray*, shrub I fancy blooms for my birthday,
reaches fullest flower, here in the Cascade foothills,
in early July. Its frothy spills of cream-white florets
those who named it must have seen
as splashes of sea-spume. There's one growing wild,
taller and fuller each year, on the rocky slope
behind this house. One at least as large
you've trained over an arbor in your garden.
There, at lower elevation, it blooms in June—
by my birthday, its hanging bunches of tiny blossoms
have already gone draggly, withered brown
as the flesh of apples in air.

Why Praise Aconites?

> *nomadic aconites*
> *that in their trek recover beautifully*
> *our sense of place . . .*
> – Geoffrey Hill

Any plant widely dispersed
will instantly recall
places we knew it before. Why
praise aconites in particular
for sounding the chords
of places we've known?

Unmistakably recognizable by how
each purple flower wraps over itself
a sort of cowl. Old garden favorites
to grow in damp shade, but infamous
across the American west
for killing cattle. They're kin
to larkspur, with a toxin that makes
eating the stalk or lacy leaves
or, especially, the root or seeds
fatal to livestock and wildlife alike.

They range, one field guide attests,
from lowland to alpland, and, says another,
from northern British Columbia southward . . .
perhaps as far as Mexico. They appear
in plant guides for eastern
North America as well as western, and Hill
must know them from England.

Their very name is nomadic—
aconite come into English
from the French *aconit,* itself derived
from Latin *aconitum,* and that,
in turn, from the Greek *akoniton.*
Their folk names, too, have passed

from tongue to tongue—French *napel*
translated to *monkshood*,
tue-loup Englished as *wolf's bane*.

Though taking different words,
the metaphors persist—they point
the one to the quaint charm
of the flower's form, the other
to the mortal harm
any part of the plant
inflicts if consumed.

Perennial herb
not only at home
in widely scattered places
of human habitation
but domestic and wild,
beautiful and potent
at once.

I'll Take These

Against a gray stone wall, masses
of small, bright mandalas—gold,
orange, and mahogany red.
A friend had planted them—
the first marigolds I truly saw, smelled,
and made my own.
Through smoky autumn haze, they glowed
the way a ginger tabby on evening patrol
seems to dispel the dusk.

Aroma of oranges, stench
of dog fennel—their odor
is somewhere between—a pungence
just this side of rankness.
Their leaves, acrid too,
are fronds—feathery, deeply cut—
so the flowers seem
what cannot be—
blossoms of ferns.

Color so vivid, scent so strong,
little wonder marigolds are strewn
on graves to draw the souls
of the dead back to earth
to feast with the living.
Though no saint is pictured
holding marigolds in her hand,
they have been deemed
worthy as riches for offering to Mary.

No landscaper would choose them
for a formal border, but,
emblems of passion, they have been
woven into garlands for weddings.
Marigolds, like me,
are most at home

in a cottage garden, slightly unkempt
at the end of the season. Crickets
scrape the background music.

By Feel

1

The August moon, ripe peach rolling
ever so slowly along
the southern horizon,
has finally slipped below
McCully Mountain's silhouette ridge.

I walk the dark house
without turning on lamps.
Only two dim night-lights
mark the hallway
with their roses of apricot glow.
It is comfort knowing
here I can find my way
by feel.

This is the season
we came here to live, dismayed to find
the green that had drawn us
when we'd come in spring
gone from the fields under parching sun.
Here, this is the season
when grass has turned sere
from dry heat
as, elsewhere I've lived,
it withers in winter from cold.
This is the season
I've been slowest to love
here.

2

Across the room
from this wingchair where I sit
to drink my morning coffee,

now hang three
watercolor landscapes:

Dark trunks, bare-branched,
rise out of snow, a distant fringe
of reed canary grass for yellow accent—
the winter woods we walked
near the Wisconsin home
we left to move here.

Beside them, reddish trunks rise
from a riot of greens—
a Coast Range creekside in spring
or fall, when the rains have returned.

In the third scene, a meadow
swells across a slope—tall grass
the color of straw, scattered with brown
seedheads of Queen Anne's lace. From low
on the left, a dirt road, half grown-over,
curves up the rise to a single
wide-limbed tree, broad crown in full
late-summer leaf. This
is the August landscape here:

clumps, mounds, and billows
of gray- and blue-greens on a ground
of bleached tan—
blackberry thickets, oaks in open stands,
hedgerows, windbreaks, woodlots
lacing, dotting, and piecing
sunburned pastures—landscape
I look on now with love
strong as it's been slow to grow.

Under the Trees

    after a painting by Ann Altman

In the shade under the trees, sheltered from the heat of the afternoon sun, the cows are not hidden. Their white faces glow against the dimness around them, as if spawn of the moon had spilled from the sky. Day after summer day, when our neighbors' Herefords chewed cud under the big firs in front of their barnyard, or under the old oaks at the far end of their pasture, I savored this scene. Now that the neighbors have reduced their herd to three, none of them Herefords, the scene returns to me on a bandana-sized square of canvas. A wide painted mat of deep purple, thickly applied, frames an inner square of summer brilliance, and that painted dazzle of sun surrounds an island of shade under trees. From there, the painted white faces of five cows, each set off by a thick outline of black, glow like so many small moons. This canvas scene now hangs beside the bedroom sliding doors, where I used to look out at the cows in the pasture below, as they sheltered from hot afternoon sun, their faces a cluster of lesser moons, glowing out from the shade under the trees.

White against Dark

> on seeing *Gardener's Gloves and Shears* (1937)
> and *Wild Roses* (1942), by Marsden Hartley

Against the dark ground you gave them,
these work gloves glow. Their frayed cuffs,
indigo blue, barely emerge
from engulfing black, but the hands—
palms up, fingers still bent
as the gardener's fingers while he worked—
have the only white in the picture, the pair of shears
rust-brown beside them.

Hartley, you had an eye
for white, bright, or pale
against dark. In this half-swathed bouquet
of *Wild Roses*, each separate
yellow-centered ragged disc
of a flower glows
rose, pink, or white against
the deep green nest of the leaves.
The paper splays open around them, blue-white
against dark red.

～

Were those gardening gloves yours? Is the shape
their painted fingers hold
the shape of your painter's hands, curved
more often to brush than to shears?
Did you use those shears to cut
the roses—not as a gift, even for yourself,
but, from the start, for a painting
envisioned already as your fingers
crimped heavy white paper around them,
laid them, wilting without water, on a table
before you, as you lifted your loaded brush
toward the hardboard propped on the easel?

No Constant Hues

Sixty years later, they still breathe
linseed oil, the petals gone over
with the gloves, the shears,
wholly to paint.

Circle, Triangle, Square

One after another, evenly spaced along the trail,
they appear at my feet: a circle of pebbles
with a larger stone at its center, a triangle of twigs,
a square, an arrow made of twigs, another of pebbles,
a twig starburst, a figure combining
arrow and square, then several more
combinations, made of both pebbles and twigs.

I imagine a purposeful child spending her whole afternoon
composing these patterns of curves and lines. First,
she picked up pebbles lying loose on the ground,
dug out some larger stones embedded in the dirt.
She gathered fallen branches. Then she sorted the stones
by size and shape, broke the branches
to a series of lengths. Kneeling on the leaf litter,
she laid out each figure in turn, standing up to get a
    good view
of her handiwork, then adjusting the position of any
awkward-looking twig or pebble, or replacing it
with another. Satisfied, she paced the distance
to the spot for the next figure and assembled it in turn—
and so on, over and over, until time to go home for supper.

She must have chuckled to herself, wondering how
    strangers
walking the trail would react when they encountered
one twig or pebble figure after another. I wish I could
    tell her
it's a pleasant surprise to discover these small works
she made, their simple shapes
amid the intricate forms of land and plants.
I'm smiling as I carefully skirt each one.

Nettlesome

Jaunty, the reddish-leafed tops poking
above the pasture grass just before
its spring spurt of growth. Dainty
red-violet flowers peer up from beneath
those mantling leaves. How
it dismayed me to learn
this plucky harbinger is
red dead-nettle, a weed. So
ominous a name and, though here
in the Pacific Northwest is where
I saw it first, no native. But not,
thank goodness, invasive, and not
dead nettle like *death* camas
or *deadly* nightshade—rather,
dead meaning *non-stinging*,
dead-nettle as distinct
from stinging nettle—

                    plant that struck
my hand with Lilliputian darts
near Mt. Damavand, Iran, tiny injections
of formic acid, the instant
I brushed its leaves. Bent on seeing
a wild red poppy, half-open behind it,
I pushed it back, thinking, *This looks
like stinging nettle, I wouldn't dare
touch this at home, but it can't
be the same plant.* It was—a weed
in North America, perhaps native
there in Eurasia. The Latin name,
Urtica, from *uro*, to burn,
is apt. Yet tradition prescribes it
for a spring tonic, and it's eaten
as a wild spinach, even cultivated
for fiber to make fish-nets and to weave

into cotton-like cloth. ... Whoever gathers
those leaves and stems must wear
thick gloves.

      Red dead-nettle
has square stems, so I knew it at once
for a mint, but my books say nothing
about its being used, like other mints,
to garnish salads, contain no accounts
of its being steeped for tea, boiled for jelly,
or packed into poultices.
Common dead-nettle, its cousin weed,
is sometimes called *henbit* because hens
reportedly nibble its leaves, but the clumps
of red dead-nettle strewing our pasture stay
untouched, small reddish islands in a wide
green sea of closely cropped grass—
both our alpacas graze carefully
around them.

        I, too, let the red-topped stalks
get leggy, prefer to pick, for my first
wild nosegays each year, the tiny violet bells
of spring queen, diminutive penstemon native
to western Oregon woods. The dead-nettles—
Lamium purpureum, little purple throats—
I leave to go to seed, but still
hold close their ruddy ardor against the chill
March rains, clutch their promise of sun.

Air on Skin

I had expected, when I returned
from Hawai'i to western Oregon's
mild winter, to settle back into
the northern hemisphere's slow
turn toward spring.
I had expected it would be enough
to watch the catkins lengthen and fatten
on the hazels, to see the spring queen's
tiny spikes of violet blooms
poke up from duff on the woods floor.
I had thought I would snuggle back,
contented, into winter wool and fleece.

Instead, I find myself yearning
for the light touch
of cotton and rayon, brushing
bare calves, for the caress
of tropical air flowing over
bare shoulders.
I pull a knit cap
down over my ears, remembering
the sunhat I wore in Hawai'i, the scent
of the white plumeria blossom
tucked in its band

I had not anticipated
leaving the islands for home
would feel like banishment.

Sometimes I remember the hottest days
of summer in a backyard that still seemed
big as the world. I remember warm air
lapping against my chest, bare
as a boy's, before I reached the age
girls had to keep
their breast-buds covered.

Windows Overlooking Gardens

Outside, and so beautiful . . .
– George Oppen

That April, spring seemed to stutter:
Daffodils budded, bloomed, died,
then budded, bloomed, and died again
when we went from Winchester to Bath.

That April, spring skipped like a broken tape player:
Daffodils barely opened,
then were gone, tulips sweeping them
off the stage, when we came from Bath to Cardiff.

Everywhere, a cold wind drove
sheets of rain. Flower-stalks bowed
beneath the wind, broke under the weight
of wet flower-heads. The gardens were still

beautiful from behind glass. Bright-winged birds
flashed through shrubbery glistening green.

Ode in Shades of Green

1

> *No white nor red was ever seen*
> *So am'rous as this lovely green.*
>   – Andrew Marvell

Though, in gardens all over the valley, camellias
are thick with white and red
globes of bloom; though the ground beneath each bush
is aproned white and red
with fallen blossoms; though, on a friend's table,
pink and purple tulips flare from a cobalt vase, and,
down street after street, full-crowned dogwoods
glow pink above azalea-brightened borders;

though the rare cardinal lobelia, its intricate
scarlet flower, lured me,
childhood summers, along banks of hidden
woodland brooks, and the radiant white
wild anemone, starring the springtime
forest floor, still quickens my breath; it's green
I would praise, green that quenches thirsty eyes
when it returns after long drought or winter freeze,

green in all the forms of leaf it takes—egg, fan,
wedge, spear, heart, and palm of hand; tender
as petals or fleshy and thick; clasping
the stem or swinging from a stalk; paired, staggered,
or set in a circlet; satin to the touch
or velvet; smooth-edged, scalloped, saw-toothed, lobed,
or cut like lace; single as thumbless mittens or split
like gloves into fingers, feathers into barbs.

Not green, but innumerable greens—golden
green of cottonwoods, newly leafed; deep teal
of Douglas firs, before bright shoots
break from their branch-tips; green lemon

of big-leaf maples' fat, dangling catkins; silvered
green of the pasture grass, mornings when every blade
is coated with dew. No constant hues, but all
continually changing as the season advances—

cottonwoods' amber bud-sap drying away,
dark firs suddenly dotted with vivid points,
emerald maples dulling in summer air,
grassblades' silver vanished in the glare of sun;
the whole palette of the landscape changing until
the green that in spring is foil for blooms
of yellow and purple, white and rose, becomes figure—
woodlots and solitary oaks scattered on tawny slopes.

2

> *Whatever is fickle, freckled (who knows how?)*
> *With swift, slow; sweet, sour; adazzle, dim . . .*
>   – Gerard Manley Hopkins

Not green, not even the sheer abundance of greens—
it's greens together, one beside another and all
    changing,
I would praise. It's greens pricked and splashed
red, white, and every pink and rose between; vernal
marshes lit with yellow spathes of skunk cabbage,
hillsides splotched with yellow broom; long vistas
of green hills receding, stepping into blue, mantled
bronze at sunset, violet in the spreading dusk.

Not green, but the lovely mottle
of red-brown dabs on the trout-lilies'
glistening fish of leaves, surfacing after rain;
not green, but the flicker
of blaze and char, as wind sways the fir-limbs;
not green, but green salad, garnished with nasturtiums,
bouillabaisse, mulligatawny, mingling hot and cool,
stew, compost, potpourri.

No Constant Hues

It's all that's stippled, checkered, dappled,
I would praise, in all its fragrance and stench.
Not only the delight when land long dormant
returns at last to green, but, equally, the ache
when the blossoms that flounced every bare twig
in the peach orchard with promise
give way to dusty leaves, when the season lurches
unstoppably onward—

Taking the Field

> *a field*
> *of the wild carrot taking*
> *the field by force . . .*
> – William Carlos Williams

They have all gone over to wild carrot—all
the fields left untilled, ungrazed, the lots
still vacant in the new industrial subdivisions,
the unmowed roadsides. And now, at this
far end of summer, all the flowers have gone
to seed, the creamy *Queen Anne's lace*
have become brown *bird's nests*, lined
each with dozens of small, bristle-covered seeds
that catch on your sleeve as you pass,
ride home with you.

                    New, each umbel lay open
to the sky, a circle of white pages around
a central spot of purple. Now they curl
in upon themselves, but still
keep casting off their bristly seeds,
poems importuning audience, insistent
on lodging in minds that will carry them
to far roadsides, sow them in distant fields.

Where Gravity Has Brought Them

Jutting out of the ground, its thin gravelly soil,
the rocks are the bones of the land,
its ribs showing, hips and elbows protruding.

Kicked loose by the hoofs of the cows as they lurch
heavily down the slopes, the rocks are great eggs
this land, once riverbed, now lays and lays.

As firs drop cone grenades on roof, deck, lawn,
as maples launch fleets of twirling propellers,
and shining flotillas sail up from thistle heads,

as blackberry canes sag with clusters of swollen
purple globules—with the same wild excess, rocks
tumble down the slopes, into heaps against tree-trunks,

into piles along the sides of steep cow-paths,
roll singly out across the flat pasture below.
There they are, like unforeseen troubles, old sorrows,

undeniable hard objects we stumble on, sometimes fall.
But, when we heft them, they fit our grasp,
worn to hand-sized roundness by the ancient river,

and, when we leave them where gravity
has brought them, they startle us with beauty,
dark gray against the ash gold of dry summer grass.

IV
Transit

High Desert Abecedarius
Oregon Star Party, August 2007

All the comforts of home
you and I and several hundred others
trade for dark skies,
for the stars as they look
far from human lights.

Brilliant, myriad,
the stars wheeling over
this sparse land
clear summer nights.

~

Cooking on our old Coleman,
I empty packets, cans,
into pots from the camping cook-set
you found abandoned in the barn.

~

Dormant since the brief
desert spring, lupine,
paintbrush, balsamroot
all look dead;
this dry plateau, desolate
until our rainforest eyes
begin to adjust.

~

East of the Cascades, broad
swaths of emptiness on the map—
we've come to one of those
empty places.

~

Forgot a nail-file.
I file my broken nails

against the rough
surface of a stone.

Ground strewn with stones—
volcanic rubble. We pry out the biggest,
then spread our ground-sheet.

Hammer we remembered—
for pounding tent stakes
into rocky soil.

Inside our tent, heat builds
all the August afternoon.
We forgot a hammock
to sling between scrub trees
where we'd have shade
and a breeze for our nap.

~

Junipers rise from this sagebrush steppe
like dark flames.
Even fallen trunks, long since
stripped of bark, still
hold the flame-twist shape
of the standing trees.

~

Kill the lights! a dozen observers
shout at once
when a car's dome-light
suddenly blazes, dazzling
their dark-adapted eyes.

Lying warm in our sleeping-bag
while you're still out observing,
I drift off on talk
of *aperture, eyepiece, NGC object*,
borne across the distance.

No Constant Hues

~

Mars, now at the closest
it ever approaches Earth,
is the brightest body
in the moonless sky.
Leaving the tent
sometime past midnight,
I see it first
by the shadows it casts.

~

Nebulae swim up
to my eye at your telescope's eyepiece
like phosphorescent fish.

Overhead, the Milky Way
stretches south to north
its luminous trail.

~

Padded in parkas for the desert night,
we'll peel down to shorts by noon.

~

Quiet surrounds
the hum of our camp—
some six hundred star-gazers
scattered across this summit.
Quickly as the desert flowers
give way to bare stalks,
all of us will leave.

~

Red-filtered flashlights
reach through the dark,
pick up the old-growth stump
that marks the porta-johns.

~

Sagebrush, bruised under boot-heels,
crushed beneath tires, diffuses its sweet
penetrant scent.

~

Telescopes, this sudden herd,
point their light-gathering
eyes at the sky all night.
Nocturnal creatures, they sleep
all day, sheathed from the heat
in aluminized mylar.

Under silvery blankets, telescopes sleep
until the dark returns.

~

Visible in the dark: worlds
daylight conceals.

~

Water from dishwashing
I pour at the base
of a scraggly tree—more than its roots
have drunk since snowmelt.
No water on this dry summit
save from a spring the Paiutes knew.
Aspen grow in its seepage, leaves
fluttering with a sound like rain.

Xeric species everywhere else, their leaves
shrunk to mere tabs, thickened,
coated with wax or fuzz—
adapted to hold moisture
through long drought.

You and I, accustomed
to humid places, would take
years to adapt. After three days,

our skin cracks, throats burn,
but we savor
this harshness
where small beauties shine
that lushness would hide.

~

Zone of rock-soil,
desiccating wind,
zone of searing summer days
and cold, dark
nights of stars,
we're ready to leave
so long as we can count on
coming back.

Transit
Pasagardes, Iran, 8 June 2004

Knee-high grass, mixed with wildflowers and weeds, spreads to the horizon—all gone to seed in the June heat. Scaffolding cages the megalithic tomb of Cyrus the Great and the giant-stepped stone plinth on which it rests. When the tomb was built, two and a half millennia ago, it rose in the midst of palace lawns and gardens. Now, these waste fields.

Amid the grass, a concrete pad, now cracked and crumbling. Here, some three decades back, the last Shah sat with his entourage, facing the great Achaemenid emperor's tomb, in a lavish celebration of twenty-five hundred years of Persian power.

Today that concrete pad is thronged. Under the blaze of the June sun, steadily climbing the sky's blue dome, some dozen Western visitors and scores of Iranians gather around a few small telescopes, all capped with solar filters and pointed sunward. Men in shirtsleeves, women sheathed in pale *manteaus* and headscarves, female students with dark *magnaehs* shrouding their hair and shoulders, all line up to peer through eyepieces as a tiny black polkadot nudges at the edge of the broad, bright disk.

No one now alive on Earth has seen this before—since 1882 no one has seen Venus move across the face of the sun. Many who watch this *transit of Venus* today will have a chance to see a second one—eight years from now, in 2012. But then the two planets will continue in their orbits for more than a century before Venus again passes between the sun and whoever will look from Earth.

The sun climbs, the heat builds, the inkspot of Venus inches along its path, ever so slowly tracing a chord across the lower third of the solar disk.

Out of the searing sunlight, beside the tour bus parked in the shade of tall trees, the bus driver and the tour guide spread out flatbread, goat cheese, yogurt, cucumbers, tomatoes, and tea—lunch or late breakfast for the Western amateur astronomers and their Iranian hosts.

On the concrete pad, in the full heat and glare of the sun, the Iranian students crowd around the visitors, especially the Americans among them, press them for autographs and email addresses, ask in careful English, "What are your impressions of Iran?" Most have never met an American before. They want to learn American English, don't know if they'll ever be able to study in the United States. Most of the Americans are visiting Iran for the first time, don't know if they'll ever be able to come here again.

~

Early this morning, in the student dorm where our group had spent the night, an Iranian man, coming face to face with me as I was leaving the lavatory in my bathrobe, head uncovered, fled down the hall as if he had seen a devil or a ghost.

A week from now, at the end of our tour of Iran, we'll make our farewells. Both the bus driver and the tour guide will flout the ban on physical contact between men and women outside the family. Each one will hug me as long and hard as if he were saying goodbye to his sister, perhaps forever.

Island Daybook

The birds talk all day here
in the foothills of Oahu's
Waianae Range, but I am silent.
I know none of their names.

~

On my hat, the five-petaled
white flower I found yesterday
nearly intact on the ground
still looks fresh, exudes a sweet,
familiar perfume. . . . Plumeria—
that's it—I had forgotten what
these fragrant blossoms were called
that island women wear
in their hair and string into leis.

~

New Year's Eve. Fireworks here
start before dusk—in Times Square, the ball
already about to drop—keep building
deep into the dark. From all along
the coast, their clamor
fills the air.

Every hour, the new year arrives
somewhere in the world.
The last hour before
it reaches here, rain
on the shingled roof overhead,
on the wide-splayed leaves outside,
begins its soft commotion.

~

Frilly red-orange blossoms
big as teacups
litter the walkways this morning—
tattered blooms
of *Spathodea campanulata*,
African tulip tree, driven down
by last night's rain.

~

Plants, birds—now the new names
swarm. I watch a pair
of red-vented bulbuls
perched amid
the dark green, lustrous leaves
of a pink tacoma. The red
is hidden under the tails
of these otherwise gray
crested birds. The color that gives
this small tree its name
appears when its dangling flowers
open the five pink lobes
of their white tubes.

~

How strange to see you here,
northern cardinal, in a coconut palm,
balmy Pacific breezes tossing its fronds—
so strange that I didn't
recognize you at first. I know you
from mainland winters, your red
brilliant against evergreens
shagged with snow. Here,
I'm strange, too. Could I learn,
like you, to thrive

on this tropical island with no
season of rest?

~

Small as New England states—
which for years were all
I knew of distance—these islands
seem mostly coast. Just a short drive
from the ocean, I reach
the ocean again.

~

I keep thinking
of the old lobsterman and his wife,
islanders off the coast of Maine,
who gave George and Mary Oppen
a tour in their pickup—
the wife telling Mary,
What I like more than anything
Is to visit other islands.

~

The woman driving
the shuttle to the airport
talks of her grown children—all
working or in school on the mainland now.
She has plans to visit them
in Arizona, Texas, Missouri.

How will she feel—born islander
suddenly landlocked
in the midst
of a continent?

V
Bright Fingers

Foothill Route

    for Richard

These back roads, country highways, winding
down from the Cascade foothills to the valley floor,
I drive just often enough to know them, just
rarely enough that almost every trip is vivid.
Each writes itself on the palimpsest of past ones,
scribing deeper and deeper the succession
of switchbacks and straightaways, blurring
scenes of sheep pasture, hayfield, fir forest,

leaving some few oddly indelible
impressions of season and weather and light:
In February's rain and early dusk, how bleak
this marginal farmland seems. . . . In May,
when hawthorns bloom in every thicket,
how my heart rides the swells of their beauty!

Most persistent of all, remembered
every time I drive this foothill route: sight
of its curves and slopes as I
never saw them, as you beheld them
the first time you took this back way home—
one winter night of full moon
and heavy hoarfrost, the road,
as you described it to me, a shining swath
through glistening hills, dazzling
and treacherous.

Softly Out of the Dark

surrounding the bed where my husband and I
lie side by side, listening on the verge of sleep, your voice
speaks from the radio on the headboard shelf, speaks
slowly, in level tones, a slightly accented English. I strain
to catch the thread, to pick up who you are—Hussein al-
Shahristani, Iraq's new minister for oil. You tell
of your success enlisting forces to protect
oil pipelines—forces that, a few months back,
were blowing them up. The BBC interviewer suggests
those fighters haven't had a change of heart—
they're protecting the pipelines largely because
your department is paying them to do so.

Then he switches topics, asks about your time
under Saddam Hussein. Slowly, softly, you tell
how you refused the dictator's order
to extract plutonium for a nuclear bomb,
how you were arrested, tortured, held
seven years in solitary at Abu Ghraib.
You had been chief scientific advisor for the Iraqi
Atomic Energy Commission—had worked your way up
in the Nuclear Research Center at al-Tuwaitha
after returning home in 1970, with a doctorate
in nuclear engineering from the University of Toronto
and a wife you'd met in the Engineering School.

Now I am wide awake—you and your new
Canadian wife must have left Toronto just after
I arrived there, with my new American husband,
keeping him with me instead of sending him off
to fight in Vietnam. Perhaps we had passed
you in the immigrant streets. Perhaps you, too,
had a flat near Bathurst, went back and forth on Bloor
between home and the university. Perhaps you, too,
ate noodles paprikash for ninety-nine cents
at the restaurant we called the *Magyar Uzlit*

even after we learned the sign in its window
meant simply "Hungarian Spoken." On campus
at Hart House, where I would stop after class
for a butter tart and tea, you went for meetings
of the Muslim Students' Association, helped
organize Friday prayers in the Debates Room.

My husband and I lie side by side, listening
together as the reporter reviews what happened
after your arrest: You were stripped naked,
hung by your wrists from the ceiling, beaten
and shocked with electric probes, for three weeks.
You say you were lucky—your wife was not raped
nor your children tortured to death
in front of you, you did not have holes
drilled into your bones, did not have your limbs
cut off with an electric saw, nor your eyes
gouged out. Your fate, you say, could have been
much worse. You talk of your time in solitary. You say
you were lucky—you did not have to witness
atrocities inflicted on other inmates. For the first few years,
you saw no one, not even the guard whose hand
delivered your meals. Then you were allowed
one visit a month from your family. Each visit,
you begged your wife to return to Canada, where she
and your children would be safe, not to stay in Iraq
through your twenty-year sentence, making
monthly trips to see you at Abu Ghraib. But she stayed.

"It seems," the reporter blurts, "you married
a strong woman." "Yes," you say. "She is strong."
She was waiting when you escaped Abu Ghraib
amid the chaos of the first Gulf War, fled with you
to Suliminiya, where you joined the Shia and Kurds
rebelling against Saddam, fled with you again
from the slaughter that suppressed the rebellion
to exile in Iran, where you worked for over a decade
defending the rights of political prisoners still in Iraq.

In the photograph my husband took of me, bidding him
    goodbye
at Toronto International Airport, when he returned
to the States to begin a new job, leaving me
to join him later, my face is bereft, full of foreboding.
How did it come to reflect anguish I had barely glimpsed?
How did all that pain of women throughout the world
gather in my face for the instant
the camera's shutter opened, to catch it on film?
I had never waited—like your Canadian wife,
Hussein al-Shahristani—at the gates of a prison
where my husband was held, never waited to hear
where he might have disappeared, never waited to learn
whether he had crossed the border safely, and found
    work,
or died in the desert. I would never wake
to my husband's nightmares of what he had suffered,
or what he had done, in war, never hear
the officer knock on the door and tell me
what his very arrival had already told.

My husband and I lie side by side. Your voice,
Hussein al-Shahristani, summons
memories of years when our lives
briefly converged with yours, before running on
in the easier course our American birth allowed.

Where I Left Off

> *We have begun to say good bye*
> *To each other*
> *And cannot say it . . .*
>   – George Oppen

Every morning I pick up
where I left off yesterday. I pick up
the magazine or book
I was reading before bed and read
the next article, the next few chapters.
I pick up the stainless steel comb
I was pulling through tangles
in our dog's long fur and pull it
through another matted patch. I pick up
the pillow case with the ripped seam
I pinned together last night
or many nights back and stitch
along the line of pins. I pick up
cards and letters that arrived
weeks ago and finally answer
the one that's waited longest.
I re-read copies of old
unanswered letters of mine, wonder
whether to send more
after them. I read aloud the poem
I've worked on each morning
for days now, try
to pick up the rhythm
of its lines, the line
of its argument. I pick up
the long conversation
I've had with you, waking beside me
now more than thirty years, wonder
what could bring me
to pick up each morning
the work I left unfinished
the night before if there were not also

our conversation, broken off by sleep,
to resume when we wake.

Lines for a Mother-in-Law

    Dorothy Buck Berry, 1916-1998

If you were here, I'd carefully skirt
November's midterm elections, which swept
your Republican conservatives from power,
regale you instead with the plants
I got to know and birds I didn't begin to learn
in two late-summer weeks on the Oregon coast,
across the continent from your Long Island Sound.
Walking Heceta Beach, beside the Pacific, I still
trailed in your wake as I had on all the walks
we took at Cove Island Park. And I'd trail you
there again, as you distinguished
every gull by species and year.

At dinner, if you were here, I'd carefully skirt
the meat you'd insist on my taking, reach
for extra broccoli, potatoes, and salad. Afterward,
when you and Dad showed slides from your
Alaskan cruise, I'd pretend to ignore
your dwelling on the fish-packing plant in Seward,
explaining every blood-smeared scene in detail,
as if to prove—as you must often have had to do,
coming of age in the '30s, sole woman earning
a doctor's degree in chemistry—that you were tough
as any man. But I wouldn't have to pretend
delight in your telephoto shots
of puffins in the Pribilofs.

And at breakfast, where I'd refuse
Dad's fried scrapple, we'd follow together
the swift forays of titmice, blue jays,
cardinals, and black-capped chickadees,
snatching seed and suet from feeders
right outside the dining-room window.
If you were here, I'd give you my annual
bird present for Christmas—say,

our friend Paul's painting of a rufous-sided towhee
perched in autumn brush, bright with ripe rosehips.
Later, in the backyard, we'd admire
the thriving growth of the copper beech
you rescued years back, a seedling doomed
to fall to the hospital ground crew's mower.

If you were alive, I wouldn't be writing you—
you hit home when you wryly complained
I wrote you so rarely your mail gave no hint
one of your daughters-in-law
was a writer. But I'd give you the poems
I've written of my slow acclimation
to the Pacific Northwest—knowing,
though you were never
a regular reader of poetry, you'd pore
over their lines, relish
all their particulars of plants and birds.

Fire All Around

      for Adrienne Rich, 1929-2012

You were too young to be my mother
I was too young to be your sister

You with hair the same auburn
as the mother I'd fled

You whose *Leaflets* pressed in my hands
by a summer school classmate
the year I'd married in June
I resisted in the conviction
poetry should stay
clear of politics

      ~

I camped on the slopes
I did not
breathe thin air and keep walking

I found
a still place in the woods
I did not
get caught up
fighting the forest fire raging around

Focused fiercely on the private
I sought only to keep
the refuge I shared with my husband
safe from the flames

      ~

Now forty-odd years
since I first read

that early book of yours
wide swaths of land have been burnt over

Some patches of forest
are black and smoking still
Underground in some places
hidden fire
smolders along tree roots

Some slopes and hollows
are stippled green
by seedlings sprouted from ash

Along the horizon new fires erupt
The air is acrid with smoke

～

I am here with my husband
in a different place
which is yet
the same place I was then
layered now with four decades
of shared life

You after years of pain
are dead
Neither daughter nor sister
I do not
follow your lead or take up your burden

But it is partly you I have to thank
no flames have forced us from
these wild fields where
we study flowers, observe the stars.

Inland from the Edge

1

Ever since I followed
the Oregon Trail west
a decade ago, I've thought I lived
at the edge where the continent
ends in ocean.
But ninety miles inland
is not the edge.

The plants are different there
or grow differently
in sea-damp air.
Not tapering tops of firs
but thick, shelving limbs
of shore pines
rear against the sky,
lean permanently eastward
beneath the prevailing
wind off the sea.

In oceanside gardens,
misted by morning fog,
fuchsias reach the size
of rhododendrons inland,
roses and dahlias sport blossoms
wide as my hand spans,
leaves the circumference of saucers
set off superabundant
gold and orange nasturtiums—
as if the land
uttered itself fully
only in the face
of ocean.

2

A friend tells me, years
before we met, when he was young
and bent on making art,
he emptied his savings
to rent a cottage on the coast
for three months. There,
working twelve hours
and eating one meal
a day, he completed almost a hundred
big still lifes, colored pencil
and cut paper, a single
huge series, mostly of flowers—

as if his carefully balanced
compositions of blooms in vases
in front of a half-closed blind,
his intricate cut-outs
of sheets of paper, spaced by heavy
sheets of glass, could hold back
the ocean. But the waves
broke in his head as they break
in a rock cave
at the edge of the land.

3

We could all
have been swept away
young, but that artist friend
now grows an inland garden,
and messages reach me
from my high school circle of rivals,
AP classmates I lost touch with
four decades ago.

From time to time, over
those years, I'd see their names—

in roundups of recent
advances in particle theory,
on the faculty roster for a top
medical school, in the music
production credits for films
that won at Sundance. Now I learn
the physicist has a daughter and son,
both in college; the research physician
worries for her mother, ninety-five,
a month in Intensive Care; the musician
has had AIDS for years, lost a lover,
dozens of friends, has more than once
been close to death himself.

Now the one whose vita
I never found on the Web
sends Williams' "This Is Just to Say"
as apology for not requiting
my story of my life
these past forty years
with a like tale of his own.

We could all have been
swept away young. I ask
about the one whose name
none of the others has spoken—
our group's irrepressible
brilliant mathematician. The answer
comes slow: *He
killed himself in college.*

4

The rest of those old classmates
get together at least
a few times a year.
They all live now
near where we grew up.
Since then I've put that place

three thousand miles
behind me. Strange to think
they stayed there, or went back,
inland from the opposite edge
of the continent between us.

The Music He Made

    Wayne Wadhams, 1946-2008

Tottering on unaccustomed heels, scanning
the room for familiar faces, wondering how
I'll look to those I seek, how they
will look to me, I could be sixteen,
dressed-up, nervous, at a party where
I've come in secret hope
the boys who see me in class
only as rival and friend will see me at last
as I dream them.

I take a plate and fill it
from the lavish array of hors d'oeuvres.
This is not the basement at Wayne's, though his
were the only parties where I was invited
and allowed to go. This is a ballroom
in the Westin Copley Boston, and the two men
who hug me awkwardly now
are sixty-plus, like me. With averted eyes,
we scrutinize each other's faces, trying to discern
what it is we find familiar despite the lines
and sagging of age.

Half a dozen of us now, together for the first time
since high school, we gather near one of a pair
of gigantic projection screens. I strain to recognize
the Wayne in the pictures, his teenage pudginess
gone, the flesh of his face looking firm,
in later shots gaunt, the wide smile
oddly persistent, as if, like the Cheshire cat's,
it existed apart. It hovers
over the room, welcoming survivors, friends
from every decade of his life. The music he made
floods from massive speakers flanking the stage,
pulses through all of our bodies.

Voices of Birds

All afternoon, while I flatten mounds
gophers have made in the lawn, and collect
upheaved stones the mower might fling
toward the windows, a low sound impinges.
For years now, I've known this soft cooing
as the song of mourning doves. Still,
half-hearing it while I rake and pick up stones,
I'm suddenly back in the yard where, only child
playing by myself, I heard it as the faint
murmur of many conversations at once
humming along the phone wires strung
from pole to pole beside the road.

~

Waking in a tent the first morning
camping in Hawai'i, I lie listening
to the loudest dawn chorus
I've ever heard. Slowly I realize
none among these many
voices of birds
is familiar.

~

Each spring at home, the familiar
songs return, one or a few at a time
swelling the seasonal choir. Not, across a span
of decades, in the same numbers; not even
all of the songs—lost to our ears as the forests shrink
that songbirds need for shelter, and we move
west and farther west.

In each new home, new songs
intrude among the known, some
recognizably similar yet distinct—of the same

family, but a different species. The move
from east coast to upper midwest brings in
the meadowlark—ravishing, unlearnable tune
I long to hear again, again—but,
over the springs there, becoming rare.
Resettled far west, it's years before I hear
a meadowlark again, heart-
breakingly beautiful as ever, but different—
of the western variety
instead of the eastern I knew before.

~

Some songs are familiar enough, have long
grown dear, but when I hear them, I fail
to picture the singer, perched on fencepost
or high branch, hidden in tall grass
or thick brush. I've never connected the song
to the species that makes it, so it stays
a tune whose composer is *anonymous*.
I dwell in the world as if on a street
where I don't know which neighbor it is
who whistles so finely as he does the chores.

~

The high end of the pitch range
goes first—so birdsong, beginning
likely with the treble notes that tell me
to scan the treetops for cedar waxwings,
companionable flocks, long since
endeared by their lingering
through all Wisconsin's winter cold.
Next, surely, the voices
of bushtits and kinglets, high
as the singers are small.
Soon, the upper notes
of the lovely melodies sung
by robins, bluebirds, and every

other variety of thrush
will vanish, too. Which beloved songs
will be the last to leave
the straining ear?

Bright Fingers

Driving west through pre-dawn dark
to arrive at the airport in time
for our early flight home, we look
back over our shoulders. . . . Remember
Rhododaktulos Eos, Homer's
"rosy-fingered Dawn"? Maybe we can catch
the tips of those bright fingers, starting
to reach up.

        So, each fall, I watch
our Christmas cactus, which, for
several years now, has bloomed
in early November, opening its first flower
on your birthday—the frilly pink
delightfully inappropriate for a man
going gray. Weeks before that day, I look
for the first tinge of red, starting to push
through the flat, segmented stalks to the ends
that will nipple into bud.

        So, each spring,
I watch, from the window above
the kitchen sink, the expectant twigs
of our shrub maple turn
brighter red each week, till they erupt
in bursts of tiny flowers, loud
with hovering bees. And every day I drive
down to the valley, I look from the car
at the peach orchard crowning
the last ridge—a chorus lifting skyward
slender arms, a haze of salmon-pink
more intense each time I pass, till they break,
all at once, into bloom.

                    Most often, it seems
it's a flush that announces
imminent transformation. But sometimes
it's pallor—green tomatoes whiten
before they turn red, as if all color
withdrew, to gather itself
for a final surge.

                    Perhaps it was such
a preparatory gathering-in
the hospice nurse saw when she called to say
your dad wouldn't last the week,
giving you just time
to get there, to interlace your fingers
with his warm, bony ones, to press
into his free hand the book of my poems
you'd brought to stand for me. He flared
to life, then sank away. Before I arrived
two days later, you and your brother
watched as his breathing
shallowed and slowed so insensibly
you almost couldn't tell
when it had ceased.

Floral Study

    for Virginia Corrie-Cozart, 1932-2012

The plant we both thought
was called *Datura* when I chose
this study of its flower from among
the couple dozen of your watercolors
you'd brought for friends to take, I read now
botanists have re-classified as
Brugmansia. Genetic analysis
keeps discovering unsuspected kinships—
we have to learn to call familiar plants
by different names.

                Your painting
shows a long, down-hung trumpet,
white with tints of cream and rose,
a fluted bud and the flared bell
of a second flower behind it. You painted it
actual size, giant blossom in close-up, pale hues
luminous against shadowy foliage,
violet dusk. Its scallop-tipped tube
bells open, half-concealing, half-revealing
its inner surface.

                A plant of this genus grows,
in a single season, into a large shrub.
An exotic, not winter-hardy here, where you
were native, but, as you recognized, beautiful
and, in the flower's form and subtly tinged pallor,
a perfect subject for watercolor.

As Lawrence took Bavarian gentians—
their great blossoms, midnight-blue—
for dark torches to lead him
downward into deeper darkness, you perhaps
saw the Brugmansia's huge, pale bloom
as a child's night-light swelled

to a full moon grazing the horizon,
casting a faint glow to comfort you
when you relinquished at last
each loved hand, face, and voice.

Left to Me

It's shadow and gleam—
this small still-life showing
a cream-painted, carved-wood chair,
drapery printed in shades
of dusty aqua and rose
spilling down its back—
faint sheen of worn threads.

Dim shape in the black
behind the chair, a table swathed
in a floor-length aqua cloth;
perched atop it, a plump
footed pot, deep teal blue.
On the floor in the foreground,
a long-necked ewer—
soft luster of old copper.

The painting is signed and dated
Charles Noel Flagg, 1908—
the artist, my maternal
great-grandfather, who painted
mostly portraits. But no one sat
for this late piece—the chair
is empty, save for the draped length
of heavy fabric.

This small canvas called *Heirlooms*—
its careful arrangement
of inherited objects,
now mine.

The Trail Down

Alone in our old
stick-shift Honda Civic, heading
south on I-5, I remember our last
car trip to Ashland, when the downgrades
left me too unnerved to drive
from Roseburg till beyond Grants Pass.

The descent beckons, said Williams, *as the ascent
beckoned*, but my palms sweat
whenever I see the sign 6% GRADE
with its silhouette picture of a runaway truck.
And summers when we hike
in the Western Cascades, I relish the climbs,

but even on slopes our favorite guidebook rates
easy or *moderate*, with only a few hundred feet
elevation gain, I still dread
losing my footing on the trail down.

The Wear

Stretched and compressed,
stretched and compressed
over and over, springs
no longer recover their shape—
metallic crystals
slip out of alignment.

Crimped by folding
again and again in the same
few ways, the skin
around mouth and eyes
no longer recovers its shape—
organic molecules
deform.

Coins that have passed
hundreds of thousands of times
from hand to hand, hand to purse,
purse to hand, are worn to smooth disks
so thin they're sharp at the rim.
The purses where the coins
have clinked, the pockets where the purses
have jounced, the hands that have plucked
the coins from the purses, slid
into the pockets and out:
all worn too—
scuffed, frayed, scarred.

Up and down the sidewalks
of the city, residents
hasten or stroll, on their way
to restaurants and shops, back
to offices and cars. The soles of their shoes
wear against the pavement; the pavement
wears under their shoes. The heels and balls
of their feet wear against the linings

of their shoes; the linings
wear against their feet. The bones
of their knees and hips
wear against each other.

Ball, rotating in socket,
wears itself down,
wears down the socket's
concave surface.
Bone, pivoting against bone,
erodes both knob and hollow.

The mechanism
no longer operates
as it once did.
The body
no longer moves
as it once did.

In Praise of Proprioception

> *proprio-* from Lat. *proprius,* one's own;
> *-ception* from Lat. *perceptio,* a receiving, gathering together

The body's own
perception of itself,
its contours and extent
within the space around it:

Body's unconscious thought,
automatic calculation,
guiding it around and through
what rises before it,

showing its hand
the way to its mouth,
allowing the stride,
the luxuriant stretch—

body's self-sense, letting
one stand beside another,
hair's breadth between them,
not touching, then touching—

when that sixth sense goes,
spinal cord's sheathing frayed,
we stagger, flail,
fall as if drunk.

What Will You Take?

The book you have re-read
every year since you read it first

at twenty? The collection of pressed
wildflowers you made as a child?

The scarf, exquisitely fine,
a friend knitted for you—

gift you hold so dear
you have never worn it?

~

Those pages your hands have turned
year upon year—will your memory

replay the text your eyes no longer
can see to read? Will your memory

call back the color long since seeped
from the pressed petals? When your hands

caress the soft wool, will your memory
conjure the hands that wove it to give you?

~

When your life that seems now
a blossoming meadow, embraced

by forested hills, companioned
by orchard and pasture,

has been left a bare width
of flinty soil, encompassed by ocean,

what will you take to the desert island
your very being has become?

The Shapes of Their Bodies

Tonight afraid that before this dark room
pales with dawn a clot will block my lungs,
I lift, one by one, the painted wooden ducks
from the shelf at the head of the bed, hold

each light body, its plump or slim form,
stroke each head, feeling the carved plumage
cleave to brow and crown, swoop back like a cap
reversed, or sweep high to a sharp edge,

trace each tail, blunt wedge or arrow
half the body's length, name them
by the identifiable shapes of their bodies:
mallard, pintail, wood duck, hooded merganser.

With death, my body, too, will be done
with the clamor and turmoil of self, will become
simply another recognizable shape
of an animal—mallard, elk, human—killed

instantly by shot or clot, stopping the heart's
quickening beat, leaving the fallen body
already beginning to fall from itself
as the sky brightens, songbirds rouse.

About the Poet

Eleanor Berry and her husband have lived in the Santiam Canyon since moving there from Wisconsin in 1994. Her earlier book, *Green November* (Traprock Books, 2007), is a collection of poems derived from her difficult acclimation to western Oregon.

A former teacher of writing and literature at Willamette University, Marquette University, the Milwaukee Institute of Art and Design, and other colleges, she is 2014-2016 President of the National Federation of State Poetry Societies and a past president of the Oregon Poetry Association, and serves on the board of the Marion Cultural Development Corporation. Her poetry and essays on poetry have been widely published in journals and anthologies.

About the Artist

Robin Christy Humelbaugh lives with her husband in rural Stayton, Oregon, where she cares for llamas, goats, and an assortment of other farm and domestic animals as well as being actively involved in the lives of her children and grandchildren.

A former dancer and dance instructor, she has been painting since the 1970s. Her innovative work in watercolor and acrylics draws inspiration from the colors and forms of the natural world. A member of the Watercolor Society of Oregon and Artists in Action, she participates regularly in paint-outs, hosts paint-ins at her farm, and teaches classes for various art organizations. Her work is regularly exhibited in regional galleries and shows.

About this Book

No Constant Hues begins with the act of seeing. And Eleanor Berry sees drama wherever she looks—in a neighbor's pasture, in a plane at 30,000 feet, in the hanging of new art work, in walking a trail, in a BBC interview, in the surroundings of an Oregon Coast Range cabin, in all that is "stippled, checkered, dappled." Her poems make celebrations of consonants and vowels: "... the azure / of sky above clouddeck or fogbank, the deep / teal of firs, umber of bark, emerald / of salal and swordfern," "... the outdoor rooms I've entered with no need to knock." Grounded in her profound affections and distinguished by a deep sense of location that extends, on occasion, to Toronto, Iran, and other distances, Eleanor Berry's generosity and patient thoughtfulness become rightness of form. *No Constant Hues* makes a fundamental reassurance that our perceptions, our thoughts and half thoughts, fears and confusions—even our calamities—might yield a clarity akin to beauty.

> – Lex Runciman, Professor of English, Linfield College; author of *The Admirations*, *Out of Town*, and *Starting from Anywhere*

Eleanor Berry has the most discerning eye for the colors and textures of nature of any poet I've encountered. I love how her poems—whether inquiries, odes, or elegies—overflow their occasions, the lush orderliness of both her landscapes and her language escaping into "wild excess." Whether recounting a thumbnail autobiography through the succession of curtains she's hung in her many windows, or considering the provenance of the stones that riddle her pasture, each of her poems succeeds in the quest for that most worthy and elusive quarry: meaning.

> – Charles Goodrich, Director, Spring Creek Project, Oregon State University; author of *Insects of South Corvallis* and *Going to Seed: Dispatches from the Garden*

No Constant Hues includes meditations on domesticity, intimacy, aging and mortality, as well as—most strikingly—meticulous observations of the natural world "continually changing as the season advances—"; as meticulously, the book is carefully stitched together line by line, poem by poem, section by section, and as a whole. One can hear and feel Berry "pick[ing] up the rhythm," as she attends to the shapes in which thought, language, and the world manifest. Here are prose poems, unobtrusive rhyme, the stepped lines of the long tour-de-force, "A Fascicle from Shotpouch Creek," even an abecedarius that one might not notice without the title because the syntax and diction in which we are told about camping out to see the stars are so straightforward. The linguistic precision works with and against the celebration of wildness, the palpable joy in the world's particularity and colors (even in "Bright Fingers," an elegy). As in the poem about reclaiming a "gravelly steep from the weeds, to hold it against further erosion," the poems are themselves "a small repair" in the earth's "tattered cover." This is a book to savor, a book that is both quiet and fierce.

> – Lisa M. Steinman, Kenan Professor of English and Humanities, Reed College; author of eight books of poetry and criticism, including *Absence & Presence* and *Invitation to Poetry*

www.ingramcontent.com/pod-product-compliance
Lightning Source LLC
Chambersburg PA
CBHW071132090426
42736CB00012B/2107